The God Who Gave You Birth

Eloise Hopkins

CW00553723

For my daughters,
Freya and Zoe,
and all those who seek.

Eloise is an artist based in Gloucester. She explores themes of memory, faith and the human
experience in her work. She is drawn to stories and beauty (found in the ordinary).

http:// elluminations.wixsite.com/elluminations/

Copyright © 2019 Eloise Hopkins

The right of Eloise Hopkins to be identified as the Author of this Work has been asserted by
her in accordance with the Copyright, Designs and Patents Act 1988.

All rights reserved. No part of this publication may be reproduced, stored in a retrieval system, or transmitted in any form or by any means electronic,
or mechanical, photocopying, recording or otherwise, without the prior permission of the publisher or a licence permitting restricted copying.

The seed of this book has been with me for a long time. It's the book I wish I'd read as a child. Growing up I learnt about 'God the Father' but never 'God the Mother'. And yet, throughout the Bible and church history, there are beautiful and powerful examples of female imagery used to describe God.

Beautiful things happen when we begin to see ourselves, in all our diversity, as a reflection of the divine. God is beyond gender and beyond language (the masculine images we have of God are largely due to the limitations of language rather than biological difference). God reveals Herself to Moses simply as "I am who I am."

To only speak of God in masculine terms limits our view of God, whether we are female or male. It does a disservice to us all. The language we choose permeates society on an unconscious level, affecting both those with faith and those without. It seems so simple that if we are all made in God's image then we all must reflect some aspect of God in our own small way. We have been unbalanced in our representations of the divine, ignoring a whole dimension of God (and in the process, marginalising half of us). The Bible speaks of equality. Jesus gave women and children a voice. This is important for all of us.

With this book I hope to make space for a fuller, richer picture of God to emerge. I have loved the process of creating these images and putting this book together. I hope to invite others into contemplation and conversation about the maternal love of God; and, in doing so, I hope that our daughters and sons and those to come will grow up with a more rounded view of the divine and of each other.

May God's blessing go with you this day.

Our Mother, in whom is heaven

Hallowed be your name

Your wisdom come

Your will be done

Unfolding from the depths of us

Give us this day all that we need

And surrender us not unto extinction

But deliver us from our folly

For yours is the beauty and the power

And all life from birth to death

From beginning to end

Give us this day our daily breath

Amen

We are all made in God's image, girls and boys, women and men. The creation story at the very beginning of the Bible tells us that…

"God created human beings, making them to be like God. God created them male and female."

– Genesis 1:27

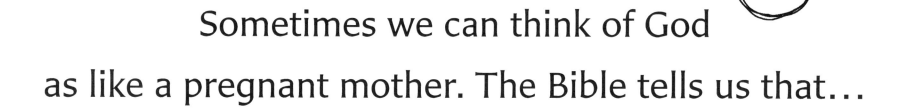

Sometimes we can think of God as like a pregnant mother. The Bible tells us that…

"In God we live and move and have our being."
– Acts 17:28

…just like a baby in the womb.

God gives us life like a Mother who gives birth.

The Bible talks about…

"…the God who gave you birth."
– Deuteronomy 32:18

And that….

"Everyone who loves is born of God."
– John 4:7

God is like a mother who feeds her baby.
God spoke to Isaiah, a prophet from long ago, saying…

"Can a mother forget the baby at her breast and have no compassion on the child she has borne? Though she may forget, I will not forget you."

– Isaiah 49:15

The Bible tells us that God is like a comforting mother, even when we are all grown up…

"As a mother comforts her child, so will I comfort you."
– Isaiah 66:13

In the Bible Moses describes God as like a mother Eagle, teaching her babies to fly. Moses taught us this song…

"Like an eagle that stirs up its nest and hovers over its young, that spreads its wings to catch them and carries them aloft."

– Deuteronomy 32:11

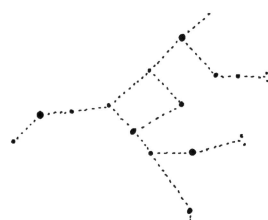

God can be fierce and strong,
like a mother Bear protecting her cubs…

"Like a bear robbed of her cubs,
I will attack them and rip them open."
– Hosea 13:8

When Jesus came along, he described himself
as like a mother hen.

*"I have longed to gather your children together, as a hen
gathers her chicks under her wings."*

– Matthew 23:37

Jesus tells a story about a woman looking for her lost coin. Jesus says that God is like the woman, comparing her joy at finding the lost coin to the joy in heaven when one person trusts and loves God.

"Celebrate with me! I found my lost coin!' Count on it – that's the kind of party God's angels throw every time one lost soul turns to God."

– Luke 15:10

The Bible tells of Jesus washing the dusty feet of his disciples. Just as a mother might bathe her child…

"…he poured water into a basin and began to wash his disciples' feet, drying them with the towel that was wrapped around him."

– John 13:5

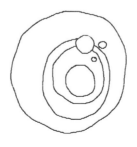

Christians throughout time have thought that God can be like a mother.

Augustine, who was a bishop from long ago, thought that God gives us exactly what we need, just like mothers do.

He wrote, *"All good things are from you, O God. Everything I need for health and for salvation flows from my God."* And, *"I (am) a creature suckled on your milk".*

And Jesus said,

"Let anyone who is thirsty come to me and drink."

– John 7:37

Way back in the 14th century, a holy woman known as Juliana of Norwich told us that

"As truly as God is our father, so truly is God our mother."

She could see that mothers can be wise and loving just like God.

She also heard God saying,

"All shall be well, and all shall be well and all manner of things shall be well".

Teresa of Avila, a Spanish nun who lived a long time ago, thought that quiet prayer can be like a mother feeding her baby because God can help us flourish without the need for words.

Teresa taught,

"Let nothing disturb you. Let nothing make you afraid. All things are passing. God alone never changes. Patience gains all things. If you have God you will want for nothing. God alone suffices."

Even when life is hard and we are sad, the Christian writer, Margaret Hebblethwaite reminds us that God is holding us close, just as a mother cuddles her crying baby.

"Just as the human mother cannot sleep while her baby is crying, so too God is with us when we feel alone or in darkness…Like the human mother she stays with us through the night hours, even if she cannot comfort us, holding us in her arms".

As we grow older we can look to God for comfort and trust that God will look after us.

"I have cared for you since you were born. Yes, I carried you before you were born. I will be your God throughout your lifetime – until your hair is white with age. I made you, and I will care for you. I will carry you along and save you."

– Isaiah 46:3

And that *nothing can separate us from God's love, not even death - Romans 8:38-39*

Additional notes

I planned this book to loosely follow the arc of life from birth through to childhood, growing up, and finally old age.

Cover – The image is of a woman with girls by her side, reaching up, searching, beseeching, receiving…

Introduction – My version of the Lord's Prayer with quotes from the following:

"Our Mother, in whom is heaven" (Ward & Wild 'Human Rites')

"Your wisdom come, your will be done, unfolding from the depths of us" (Patricia Lynn Reilly)

"Give us this day all that we need" (Daniel Charles Damon)

"And surrender us not unto extinction, but deliver us from our folly, for yours is the beauty and the power, and all life from birth to death, from beginning to end" (Henry Horton)

"Give us this day our daily breath" (My daughter, Freya)

Page 6 – Based on the landscape of Africa and referencing the first people. In the Bible translation, I've replaced the word 'he' with 'God'. (Good News translation).

Page 8 - This artwork conjures pregnancy images for me - the space person, complete with 'umbilical cord' staring out into the wonder of the universe. I deliberately left the space person as outline only; we are all made of stars after all! In the Bible quote I've replaced 'he' with 'God'. (NIV translation).

Page 10 - I have taken cave art as inspiration to illustrate the birth of humanity and indeed all life on our planet. I had words from a Rilke poem running through my head whilst creating this, "flare up like a flame and make big shadows I can move in."

The handprints come from real people, from friends and family, and the circles and lines around the woman are taken from an aboriginal symbol for 'meeting place' but can also be seen as a halo. (NIV translation).

Page 12 - The woman here is feeding her baby and also a Sunbird, indicating that God loves and nourishes all of creation. She is sat by a Banyan tree – they "root themselves to form new trees and grow over large areas. Because of this characteristic and its longevity, this tree is considered immortal and is an integral part of the myths and legends of India." (Wikipedia & NIV translation).

Page 14 – It's helpful and comforting to show images of maternal love and care continuing past the baby phase. This artwork shows me as a grown up with my mother; the image is especially poignant for me because my mum died while her children were still young. (NIV translation).

Page 16 – The process of making this image involves using layers. When I lay the original image flat you see only the person, but when I hold it up to the light it reveals the image of the bird carrying her. A great image for God who we can't see but is sometimes unexpectedly revealed. (NIV translation).

Page 18 - This image is based on my daughter, 7 years old at the time. In her own imaginative play she conjured the image of 'Fierce Antler Woman'. It's so important that we show rounded versions of childhood - Girls, and women can be fierce. This painting offers a challenge, you have to come face to face with the fierceness before travelling beyond. The constellation in the sky behind her is based on Ursa Major, which is also known as 'The Great She Bear', referencing Hosea's image of God as a fierce, protective, mother bear. The constellation is also used in navigation and points to the Pole Star. (NIV translation).

Page 20 – I had fun illustrating a hen taking care of her brood. I took inspiration from a charcoal sketch by Susan Cook. The round shapes under her wings can be faces or eggs, and they each have a different expression, because we're all different! (NIV translation).

Page 22 – I decided to paint an older woman's face as I planned the book to include different phases of a woman's life. (The Message translation).

Page 24 – I was searching for a new way to illustrate this well known passage. The chosen angle can help to see the story in a fresh way, and the stylised water gives space to think of it as more than just water. (NIV translation).

Page 26 - I like to imagine Communion as God gathering us around Her table and feeding us with what we need to help us flourish. A friend of mine, who is a vicar, told me that when she was pregnant, presiding over the Communion table was a particularly powerful experience for her. As a pregnant mother you are feeding the child within you with your own body. I took inspiration from my friend's (another vicar!) stole depicting Martha and the Dragon in this image. Rather than killing the beast, Martha tames it, pointing to a different way of being and working, one that I think women often bring with them. (Augustine quote from 'Confessions' & NIV translation).

Page 28 – Juliana (also known as 'Julian') of Norwich is strongly linked to cats and is often depicted with a feline companion. This is probably because she secluded herself away from other people in order to live a life of prayer. Her only companion was a cat. (Quotes from Juliana of Norwich's 'Showings' and 'Revelations of Divine Love').

Page 30 – We often need to speak, to explain ourselves, to get our point across; but with God, no words need be said, God understands and responds. Just like a mother responds to her baby's needs without the need for words. In fact, breast milk often changes in response to subtle cues from the baby so that it provides exactly what the child needs at the time. The image came about after quiet prayer, realising that I didn't need to say anything to be understood. A friend reflected that the fire illustrates being drawn to the heart of God. (Translated from Teresa of Avila's poem 'Nada Te Turbe').

Page 32 - I prefer this image as an alternative to the famous 'footprints' poem. I like that it acknowledges that sometimes the pain remains, even if God is with us. Just like when we cuddle our distressed baby close, the baby may not stop crying but we are willing the discomfort to ease and loving them through the difficult times. (Quote from Hebblethwaite's 'Motherhood and God').

Page 34 – A friend, Tim Hutchinson, took a photograph of curls of smoke, when he developed the image he realised the smoke had formed the shape of a woman, perhaps a pregnant mother. I fell in love with the image and wanted to use it in this book. The image can be enjoyed as it is, but the layers of meaning invite us into a deepening understanding and relationship with our creator. The smoke is insubstantial and impossible to grasp, but it briefly shows us a pattern, a picture of a pregnant mother. The image is perfect for the last page, it speaks of coming to the end of our life, approaching the unknown, but being sure of God's enduring love and ability to bring life from death, to make all things new. In an alternative image (see below) I added pinpricks of light forming a crown around her head. The dots and dashes spell out 'El Shaddai' in morse code, one of the Hebrew names for God that can be translated as 'All Sufficient'. (New Living Translation).

With thanks to G and all those who journey with me.
Our evolving conversations and relationships carry me further round the spiral each time.

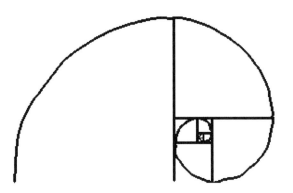

CPSIA information can be obtained at www.ICGtesting.com
Printed in the USA
BVIW121029050919
557658BV00011B/68

* 9 7 8 1 9 0 8 8 6 0 9 9 6 *